Disney · PIXAR
RATATOUILLE
(rat·a·too·ee)

Level 5

Re-told by: Mo Sanders

Series Editor: Rachel Wilson

Contents

In This Book

Remy

A young rat who loves to cook

Emile

Remy's brother who lives in the sewer with the other rats

Linguini

A young man who works in the kitchen of a famous restaurant

Chef Skinner

The top chef at Gusteau's restaurant

Colette

A young chef who works at Gusteau's and helps Linguini

Anton Ego

A restaurant critic who frightens many of the chefs in Paris

Before You Read

Introduction

Remy is not like all the other rats—he loves to cook! He goes to Paris and finds the restaurant of a famous chef. There, he meets a young man called Linguini, who works in the kitchen. Remy helps him to make delicious food. But what will Chef Skinner say about a rat in his kitchen? What will Anton Ego, the most frightening restaurant critic in Paris, think about Linguini and Remy's food? There are always going to be problems in a world where people hate rats.

Activities

1 **Match the words and the pictures. You can use a dictionary.**

waiter   customer   critic   cookbook   pot   chef

A

B

C

D

E

F

2 **This book is called *Ratatouille*. What do you think "ratatouille" is?**

1 A Different Kind of Rat

Remy was different than the other rats. They were happy to eat old food, garbage … *anything*. But Remy loved food. He loved to taste new things and he could smell everything! Remy had a brother, Emile. They were very different, but they were best friends. Emile thought Remy had talent.

Remy's father, Django, didn't understand Remy and said, "Eat your garbage."

Remy didn't listen. Sometimes, he went into the kitchen at night and read the cookbooks.

Remy's favorite cookbook was by Chef Gusteau. One night in the kitchen, Remy saw the famous chef on TV. But it was bad news: Gusteau was dead. Remy couldn't believe it.

Suddenly, the woman of the house woke up and saw him. "Ahhh!" she cried. Humans hated rats—it was time to leave!

The rats ran down to the river and jumped into their boats. Remy ran, too, but it wasn't easy to run with the cookbook.

"Come on!" Django called to Remy.

The cookbook was Remy's boat. He tried to follow the others along the river and the sewer. But he lost them in the fast waters of the sewer.

The water carried him along for hours. At last, his boat stopped. With no family or friends, Remy sat and read the book. He felt hungry and sad. There was a picture of Gusteau in the book. Suddenly, Gusteau spoke to him! "If you are hungry, go up and look around, Remy," he said.

Remy decided to leave the sewer. He climbed up into the building above

It was full of humans, but Remy was careful. He climbed higher and higher until he was at the top. From there, he could see the whole city at night.

"Paris?" Remy said in surprise. "Wow. It's *beautiful!*"

There was a big sign on the building opposite him. It was Gusteau's restaurant. This was Remy's dream come true!

"I have to see this," said Remy.

2 Linguini's Soup

Remy looked down through the window. He watched the chefs at work in the kitchen below.

Not all the people there were chefs. It was the job of one tall boy to take out the garbage. He was near a pot of soup when his arm hit it. Some of the soup fell out. The boy looked around quickly. Then he started to put water and other ingredients into the pot.

"What is he doing?" cried Remy. That wasn't the way to make soup!

When Remy shouted, he fell through the window and down into the kitchen.

A busy kitchen in a restaurant was a dangerous place for a rat! Remy ran for the window as fast as he could, before any chefs saw him.

He stopped when he was near the soup. He could smell it. Salt! That soup didn't have enough salt! Or pepper ... or spices. Remy forgot about the danger and started to cook.

The tall boy returned. His mouth opened in surprise when he saw Remy cooking.

Suddenly, an angry voice shouted, "Where is the soup?" It was Chef Skinner. After Gusteau died, the restaurant became Skinner's.

Skinner didn't see Remy, but he saw the garbage boy holding a large spoon. "You are cooking? In *my* kitchen!"

The soup was already on its way to a customer.

"STOP THAT SOUP!" shouted Skinner. But it was too late.

"Linguini!" screamed Skinner, "You're fired!"

When the waiter returned, the chefs waited for the bad news.

"What did the customer say?" asked Colette, a young chef at Gusteau's.

"It wasn't a customer. It was a critic," said the waiter. "She liked the soup!" he cried.

"Umm, am I still fired?" asked Linguini.

"You can't fire him," said Colette to Skinner.

Skinner tasted the soup. It was good—delicious! "You will make the soup again," he told Linguini, "And this time I'll be watching you!"

Remy didn't want to stay in the kitchen. He was nearly at the window when Skinner saw him.

"Rat!" cried the chef angrily. "GET IT!" All of the chefs moved fast. Remy tried to run, but Linguini caught him.

"What shall I do with it?" he asked.

"Take it away from here, far away," shouted Skinner. "Kill it. Go!" Linguini ran outside and quickly rode his bicycle to the river.

3 A New Way to Cook

Linguini couldn't throw the rat into the river.

"I need this job," he said sadly. He only had the job because his mother was Gusteau's friend. How could he cook the soup again?

"I don't know how to cook and now I'm talking to a rat—wait a second. Did you … just move your head?" he cried, looking at the rat.

The rat's head moved—yes.

"You *understand* me?" Linguini asked.

Again, Remy's head moved—yes.

Linguini had an idea. "I can't cook. But you can!"

Linguini took Remy back to his little home. But how could the rat help the human to cook?

Remy had the best idea. He sat on Linguini's head and held two pieces of hair. When Remy pulled the left piece of hair, Linguini moved his left hand. When he pulled the right piece, Linguini moved his right hand.

Then they just had to practice for hours and hours. After a lot of practice, Remy could control Linguini's hands. Now he could cook!

Remy and Linguini were ready to make the soup again for
Chef Skinner.

    In the restaurant kitchen, Remy hid under Linguini's hat.
He remembered the words of Chef Gusteau and controlled everything.
With Remy's help, Linguini made the soup again.

    When the soup was ready, Skinner tasted it. The soup was good.
Skinner didn't really want Linguini in his kitchen, but now he had to
keep him. He told Colette to help Linguini.

Linguini made the same soup every day with Remy's help, and the customers loved it. But one day, a customer wanted a *new* dish.

Skinner chose an old Gusteau recipe and told Linguini and Colette to make it.

It was the only Gusteau recipe that didn't work. Gusteau hated it! Skinner knew that. He wanted the dish to be terrible. Then he could send Linguini away from his kitchen.

"I don't know this recipe," Colette said, "but it's Gusteau's."
She told Linguini to follow the recipe.

From under Linguini's hat, Remy looked at all the ingredients.
This recipe was terrible, so he decided to change it.

Colette was angry, "What are you doing?" she shouted at
Linguini. But it was too late. The customer already had the meal.

The waiter returned. "They love it!" he cried.

"That's … wonderful," said Skinner, unhappily.

4 Family and Friends from the Past

After work, Remy went outside behind the restaurant. He felt tired, but also happy—the customers liked his cooking!

Suddenly, he saw a dark shape near the garbage. There were two red eyes in the night. Remy was afraid, but then …

"Remy!" Emile jumped into the light. "You're alive!"

"Emile?" Remy was so happy to see his brother again.

"Dad doesn't know you're alive. We have to go!" Emile cried.

"You're home!" Django cried. He was so happy to see his younger son again.

Remy tried to explain about his new life, how he liked working in the restaurant.

Django was angry now. "You're not staying?" he asked. Django didn't want his son to live around humans—they only wanted to kill rats.

"No, Dad," said Remy quietly. "It doesn't have to be that way." He turned and walked away.

Remy returned to the restaurant. Then Emile came there with some friends. They wanted him to steal food from the restaurant.

"You told them, Emile?" Remy was angry, but he agreed to do it just once.

He ran inside to Skinner's office. Where was the key for the storeroom? Remy found the key in Skinner's desk—he also found some papers in there. One was from Chef Gusteau, before he died. The other was a letter from Linguini's mother, Renata.

Renata's letter explained that Linguini was … Gusteau's son! And Gusteau's letter explained that any child of his gets his restaurant when he dies. Remy looked up. Linguini didn't know it, but Gusteau's restaurant was his, not Skinner's!

Suddenly, the door opened. Skinner was there! But Remy was much faster than the chef. He ran out of the office with the papers in his mouth. He had to show the papers to Linguini.

5 The New Star of the Restaurant World

As soon as Linguini saw those papers, his life changed. Chef Skinner had to leave quickly before the police caught him.

Now the restaurant was Linguini's, and he was the star of the Paris restaurant world. All the newspapers wanted his photo for their front page. They all wanted to write stories about the great new food at Gusteau's restaurant. Linguini happily answered all their questions about cooking. He liked being famous!

Remy just stayed under Linguini's hat and listened.

Suddenly, a tall, thin man came into the restaurant. All the people became quiet. This was Anton Ego. He was the most famous restaurant critic in Paris. Every chef in the city was afraid of him. Ego only ate the best food. When he didn't like a restaurant, he wrote a bad review in the newspaper and the restaurant closed!

Ego looked at Linguini now. "I will return tomorrow night," he said.

Remy was unhappy. People loved the restaurant now and Linguini was famous. But Linguini wasn't really the chef, Remy was! Linguini also felt bad. Remy wasn't the only chef with talent. "Colette knows how to cook too, you know," he said.

From under the hat, Remy pulled Linguini's hair too hard. "Ow! All right, that's it!" cried Linguini angrily. He walked outside the restaurant. He wanted some time away from Remy. Linguini put Remy down and went back into the restaurant.

Outside the restaurant, Remy found his brother. More of Emile's friends were with him now, and they were all hungry.

"I'm sorry, Remy," said Emile, looking at the rats.

Remy was still angry with Linguini, so this time he didn't stop to think.

"You know what? It's okay. Are you hungry?" he asked the rats. Yes, they were all hungry!

"We'll go after closing time," Remy said. "Tell Dad to bring all the rats!"

Later that night, Remy led the rats into the restaurant kitchen and showed them the storeroom.

Suddenly, there was the sound of feet—human feet. The rats hid just before Linguini turned on the light. Only Remy stayed out on the kitchen floor.

Linguini looked down at his little friend. He was sorry. "I don't want to fight," he said. "You're always here for me, you help me …"

From a corner of the kitchen, Django heard everything that Linguini said.

Linguini went to the storeroom and turned on the light. There were rats everywhere.

What was happening? Linguini turned to Remy, "You're stealing from me? How could you? I thought you were my friend! Get out and don't come back!"

Hundreds of rats ran from the kitchen, and Remy ran with them. It was nearly time for Anton Ego to arrive. Linguini had to cook the most important meal of his life … *without* Remy!

6 The Most Delicious Meal

When the other chefs arrived, Linguini was nervous. He was more nervous when a waiter said, "Ego is here!" Linguini didn't know what to do. He couldn't cook without Remy.

Suddenly, Remy was back! Then Colette saw Remy, "Rat!" she cried.

"Don't touch him!!" shouted Linguini. He picked up Remy and told them that the rat was the secret chef. "I have no talent at all. This rat is the real cook!" said Linguini.

The chefs left. They didn't want to work with a rat! But Linguini and Remy couldn't cook for Ego without the other chefs.

Suddenly, Django was there. "I was wrong about your friend. And about you," he told his son.

Then Django called, and the kitchen was full of rats, ready to help. "We're not cooks but we are family. You tell us what to do and we'll get it done."

First, the rats got clean, then they got busy.

Colette felt bad, so she came back. She was surprised to see the rats in the kitchen and Linguini working as a waiter!

"Just tell me what the rat wants to cook," she said. Remy showed her a recipe. "Ratatouille? Are you sure?" she asked Remy. It was too easy!

But Remy's Ratatouille was different. When Linguini brought him the dish, Ego just looked at it. He tasted the vegetable stew. Then he smiled. It was … wonderful!

After dinner, Ego asked to meet the chef. When the last customer left, Linguini and Colette brought Remy to the table. No more secrets, they decided.

At first, Ego didn't believe them, so they took him to the kitchen. They showed Ego how they worked.

The next day, Ego wrote his review of the restaurant. He gave it five stars!

"A great artist can come from anywhere," he wrote. "The chef at Gusteau's is the finest chef in France."

After You Read

1 **Choose the correct answer.**

1 Remy lost his friends and family in ...

   a the house   **b** the sewer   **c** the restaurant

2 Remy controls Linguini with ...

   a the chef's hat   **b** a cookbook   **c** his hair

3 Linguini is ...

   a Renata's son   **b** Chef Skinner's son   **c** Colette's brother

2 **Complete the sentences with the correct phrases.**

1 Remy makes the soup ...

2 Linguini takes Remy to the river ...

3 Remy teaches Linguini ...

4 Remy sees an important letter ...

a in Skinner's office.

b at Linguini's apartment.

c on his bicycle.

d in the restaurant kitchen.

3 **Read and discuss. Which of these sentences is NOT a main idea in the story?**

1 It is good to try new things.

2 People can change.

3 Always stay with your family.

4 You can find talent in surprising places.

29

Glossary

alive (*adj.*) a person or animal which is living; the opposite of dead

control past tense **controlled** (*verb*) to make a person or thing do something that you want them to do; *After a lot of practice, Remy could control Linguini's hands.*

delicious (*adj.*) very nice to taste or smell; *Remy helps him to make delicious food.*

fired (*adj.*) when you lose your job because you did something wrong

full (*adj.*) with a lot of people or things inside; *It was full of humans, but Remy was careful.*

garbage (*noun*) the things that people throw away

human (*noun*) a person

ingredient (*noun*) one of the foods that you use to make a meal

key (*noun*) a small piece of metal that you use to open a door or start a car

meal (*noun*) the food that you eat for breakfast, lunch, or dinner

news (*noun*) information about something that just happened

recipe (*noun*) something that tells you how to cook a meal

return past tense **returned** (*verb*) to come or go back to a place; *I will return tomorrow night.*

review (*noun*) words that a person writes about a restaurant, book, or movie, for example; it tells people how good a place or thing is

salt (*noun*) something that you can put on food to make it taste better

secret (*noun*) something that not very many people know about

sewer (*noun*) an underground road that people build to take water away from towns and cities

sign (*noun*) something on the outside of a building that tells you the name of the place

stew (*noun*) a hot meal, usually with meat and/or vegetables; you cook it for a long time

talent (*noun*) something that a person can do very well

Play: Good Food Is Important

Scene 1:

Emile and Remy are outside. Emile is eating something.

REMY: What are you eating, Emile?

EMILE: I don't really know. I found it in the garbage.

REMY: What? No! Don't eat bad food—eat good food!

        [Remy takes the food from Emile and throws it on the ground]

Scene 2:

Emile, carrying a bag in his mouth, sees Remy, who is carrying a mushroom.

EMILE: What do you have there, Remy?

REMY: It's a mushroom. I found it in the forest.

        [Remy smells the bag and smiles]

        And what do you have in your food bag, Emile?

EMILE: Only a piece of cheese. I found it in the garbage outside the house.

REMY: [with hands in the air, looking pleased]

        We can make a fantastic meal with *my* mushroom and *your* cheese.

Scene 3:

Remy is cooking the cheese and mushroom together and Emile is watching.

REMY: Smell this, Emile. It's going to be *delicious*!

EMILE: [laughing kindly] If you *say* so!

Global Citizenship

Food Waste Is Bad for People and the Planet

Many people in the world are hungry—but we waste about one-third of all the food that we make. Growing and making food takes a lot of land, water, and energy. When we waste food, we also waste these things.

We can reduce our food waste at home by thinking before we buy, and by choosing and eating carefully!

✔ Plan meals for a week and only buy the food that you can use.
✔ Store food carefully.
✘ Don't cook more than you can eat.
✘ Don't throw away leftovers. There are many good recipes for them.

World Food Day happens in October every year so that people can learn how important food is.

How do you cook ratatouille?

Ratatouille is a famous French dish. It first came from Provence, in the south of the country.

Every chef has his or her idea about how to make ratatouille. There are many different recipes, with different ingredients and cooking times. Here's one quick and easy recipe for ratatouille that you can make with an adult.

INGREDIENTS
- 1 onion
- 2 pieces of garlic
- 1 eggplant
- 2 zucchinis
- 2 bell peppers
- 4 large tomatoes
- herbs
- oil for cooking

Chop the onion and garlic into small pieces. (Ask an adult to help you chop the vegetables.)

2

3

Put the oil in a pan. When the oil is hot, put the onions and garlic in the pan. (Always be careful when you are cooking.)

Chop the other vegetables. When the onions and garlic are soft, put the vegetable pieces into the pan. Cook for five minutes.

4

herb

Chop the tomatoes and herbs and put them in the pan with the other vegetables. Cook for 30–40 minutes.

Eat your ratatouille with some good bread.

Phonics

Say the sounds. Read the words.

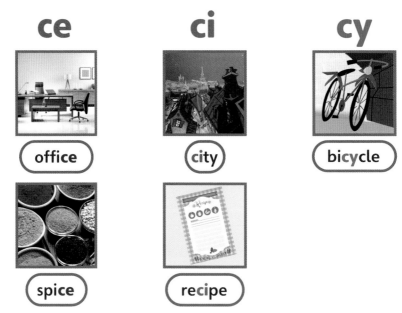

ce
office

spice

ci
city

recipe

cy
bicycle

Read, then say the rhyme to a friend.

I went there once, I went there twice.
The food's delicious, more than nice!
The city's best restaurant, I must say.
And you could race there now, today!

Jump on your bicycle, quick, and ride,
Then try the food and you decide.
And tell me, look me in the face—
Is this the city's finest place?